The Scene You See

Joannie Stangeland

Joannie

To Emily —
Best wishes
for your writing.
In the art
of always, J.

May 17, 2018

Cover image: "Le peignoir bleu" by Henri Lebasque, in the public domain

Also by Joannie Stangeland:

A Steady Long for Flight
Weathered Steps
Into the Rumored Spring (Ravenna Press)
In Both *Hands* (Ravenna Press)

FIRST EDITION

ISBN: 978-0-9995921-6-8
LCCN: 2018937630

Published by
Ravenna Press
(ravennapress.com)

Contents

iii. of a feather

For Tom

I am just beginning to understand what it is to paint.
A painter should have two lives, one in which to learn,
and one in which to practice his art.
-Pierre Bonnard

i. hunger-drunk

.

Self-Portrait with an Aubade

The light must be sheer—Vermeer's *camera obscura*
draws early sun, gauze filtered
through green. Leaving shadows' blue pools,
       night's voices vanish.

Water jug, leaded glass, and ultramarine,
morning streams a sacrament—thin blessing
melts before you swallow. Tension subtle,
       serene across the canvas.

Look to the window when day brushes your face,
clean strokes—the care, translucent.
Step into this skin like an artist, a flautist,
       a muse. A yellow cup.

Place your eye in the middle.

Time and Materials

To feel the sweep of chalk, dry scuff—
the sidewalk's artist kneeling by Washington Square—

To stroke the clay's story thrown and slipped
through hands, shaping air inside the pot.

Rub the silks and yarns—one nubbed
wool leaves its oils on open palms.

Tell the lives the sticks of charcoal led,
their green pasts a tree across a page.

Trace voices birds throw against
the sky, songs drawn, spectral. A door

opens. Light leaves its legends everywhere.

~~~

To know like breathing the way the brush runs
across the canvas, how paper drinks the wash
and each color meets another—Madder,
Cobalt, all Cadmium. How we learn
our bodies, that intimacy—call and response.

To study deeply, rush to saturation,
and the light its own music. Vision bends
through old window glass, fountain splash,
a shade below the leaves. I gulp the air,
practice inspiration, the sky its own art.

I sink into blue, and the hours barely help.

~~~

The lines on my palms a story I can't read—
the smell of ice or morning before it snows,
fog brushed gray, clouds falling.

I'll vanish with you somewhere west, perspective
crossing longitudes—every past a picture
and the light yellow sunk before a storm.

Paint me potato stew. Draw me a drink.
Name each flavor to me, with salt.
I'll taste. I'll toast you. How much tonic? And who?
Clink me this perfect hour, closing to dusk.

~ ~ ~

It wasn't the kitchen garden, that first Paradise,
miracle told from mother to child at her knee
whites washed with bluing, lemon juice.

Lilies didn't spin, but women toiled
with curses under their nails and the color red—

Eden, as in a painting by Rousseau.
Green's lush suggestions flesh the fronds,
the sun that must be setting, and in the middle

a brocade length of snake, apple in its fangs,
and the woman bare, hand open, ready
to be beautiful—now what to make for supper.

~ ~ ~

Let me peel onions without crying,
garlic heads and then the leeks—
the aromatic palette stings,
brings the tears before the meat.

Let me taste the dirt that swallows seeds
and bulbs, roots and the dead. The body becomes
another body—splits in smallest measures,
cells returning to earth, to leaf, to air,
rambling atoms. Here, we breathe our past.

~~~

Oh, embrace—Oh, molecular structures,
grave physics of time and spark! In the dark
I feel empty. Tonight the full moon
will pull me apart, riptides sucking hours
and salts—secrets thick in a dog-eared atlas,

Oh, eddy—a shushing drum in my ears.

Stars jam the canopy—dust to burn.
I turn to fold my hands, a prayer or a cup.
To make the mind see its vision finished—
its little god moment, and the art unravels.

The light a stage, a world and a door to that world.

A Tree That Looks Like a Tree

I wanted to paint the way wings feather air,
how shadows shiver walls when the wind
finds its brush, to make the waves the sun leaves.

To shade an afternoon raises questions
of gradation—the sky teal to blue,
an ochre bowl with apples or lemons.

If I would be an artist, could I find
the path from palm to cloud, translate
from eye to hand to line, and then the birds?

I sat in class, drew the Mayor's daughter.
Later, my shirt's flannel folds—
charcoal smudging the shadows soft.

I faltered, didn't see past the surface,
how a teacup could become a flying saucer.
The tree stayed a bouquet of lemons

Hostage to my sad hands, I'm left
looking for words to pull from dry air,
my blank page another white flag.

Another Supper Finds Me Lost

I gouge out the eyes of the oldest red potatoes—
what grows below ground waits
to bring its dirt to light.

Carrots and half an onion replace pastels.
Root names nourish my tongue.
I hunger. How to eat all day—

fill the pot with water, start the flame.
My lover, the artist, arranges every plate,
porcelain canvas sauced and garnished.

My dinners more Grandma Moses,
folk art in the kitchen, warm in the mouth
and the deep empty I haven't filled—

the chalks in their box, *maybe*
stashed under the bed, agreement scrapped
by eyes and the brain that speaks to my fingers

a different dialect, message stuttered.
A child opens and closes his hands, lights
turning off and on. His language—*I want.*

Between the knife and board
my vision's tossed aside for bread.
Steam swamps the window, the green beyond.

Give me subtle flavors, shades of bay,
the late sun's dusty veil—a figure
in the next room, the table set for two.

Diptych with Limited Symptoms

My body—shrine or haunted house
dark in its alcoves, hidden stairways
behind closet doors. From horror

to mistrust—lust, fatigue, the lush
thirst without knowing what is made
and unmade, failures and wear, each
room a denouement—and then

the clock spits minutes. The eyes
give the brain everything as ghosts,
bone scaffolding stands askew.

~~~

I know better, and yet no longer
trust my hands to turn the knobs.

Oh body—how I betray you,
each day another promise
dropped like a glass on tile.

Sweep up my pieces. Plant a lilac
in my mouth and let the roots plumb
my organs, muscles, vessels—yes,
tendril my bones, and feel me blooming—
Oh, anxiety, changing costumes.
Give me a hat that fits, and a ribbon.

Self-Portrait with Biscuits

I was easy—in butter and honey I swallowed
all the shades of morning, spread my paints
rushed, indulgent.
          I overlooked the colors,

missed the lines, one more mistake.
I swept crumbs into my palms, eager
to eat—my little luxury—
          better than chasing

this dough face that hides from her own eyes.
I set the brush in the sink, wash the knife,
the white plate,
          an aftertaste,

and too much cream.

Appetites

I love the light almost as much as the biscuit
on my plate, having given up jam and butter,
but the sun I drink with my cup of coffee brings me
heat and no guilt by association,

acquaintance with my middle age—the spread
I struggle against, vanity mixed with sanity.
My head sticks to one story, my gut
another ending.

        I pretend I've paid for this morning
flight from rain, to sprawl in the desert,
watch shadows shift—

        I'm a sunflower,
Van Gogh's *tournesol* to track the fire
across a day, pray I don't burn.

~~~

Across the day burning, I pray to swallow
simple seeds. If I could learn like a bird,
day-long forage, peck and graze.

I savor the light like a bouquet. Chardonnay,
gold nuance in a glass. How many ways
can I consume—more—and be embraced?

I leave the news to you to cover, tell me
local stories when I've returned from the garden.

Call me shallow, I'm drying up and I make
no excuses. Another hunger to fill,
words on other pages. Sage advice

with salt. I'm low altitude, high maintenance.

~~~

Let me pen my dramas in my lowest Hell.
Leave a plate of cheese, lemon vodka.
I sour long, ferment for dusty sun.

I trust the clock doesn't run faster,
hands awhirl like children reaching dizzy.
I don't like the spinning.

       Or this vision—
tree from the backyard and my young self
in a blue jacket, knee-high as the world
twirled around. This fixed in my head

like an envelope stuffed in a desk, pigeon-holed
and I'm the flea-bitten bird in my own hand,
no parable of doves or bleeding saints.

~~~

Faith a market pierced and cornered by the saints,
but I've heard about the Frenchman in the bar
painting them all in his likeness, his face on the canvas,
bodies speared by arrows, pocked with pestilence—

now he's in his fifties he finds and feeds
this new motif, and sleeps through the early mass.

The story goes he sailed to his usual table
surrounded by believers—women as supple
as brushes, blending into the sable evening
and ice in glasses.

       In Paris, one understands
how to sate all appetites.
One understands the way to love the light.

Self-Portrait, if I Were Bonnard

You find the window framed, morning beyond.
I gaze through panes, pauses, but I'm not
                                    in the picture.

The scene you see is what you meet of me.

Not the curtain long on the left edge.
Not the blue cloth on the table, the bowl

of oranges, but this lemon light implied

through glass, this honeyed life that looks out
over the trees, vantage point on vanishing.

Noon's brash pigments are hours away.

Shadows change their dresses, shift relief

under the paint's skin—illumined, gold
desire stippled to trick the eye, the sun

a gift, and this the best of me.

This Shade So Early Clings

After Le Peignoir Bleu, *by Henri Lebasque, 1920*

Night rinsed pale as watercolor stars
lifts above your shoulders, vanishes

beyond that lilac mountain, your morning framed
by sheer curtains, the balcony's iron ornament,

but past the window, the trees' green and a sky
that washes softer than blue, nearly clear
to inspire, inhale, one cloud enough

to make you see a lucky rabbit,
a duck the dawn pearls and leaves.

You strike a bargain, feel the sun
stroke your throat as the world opens

like a shell, or the peephole in the egg you saw as a girl,
glimpse of a meadow in miniature,

memory breathing still beneath your ribs,
the dream that hovers, dust in the light.

Below, the cat snakes ankles
for cream or a fish head.
Birds begin their arias again.

When you hear a child sing, you'll slip
this cobalt robe and quiet, join the hours on the ground,
the day's aches and taxes.

Self-Portrait, if I Were Lebasque

Light, light—a river.
Cast an eye for shadows. Here, the *Midi*
heat wraps my bones like gauze and bliss
    disconcerts my critics.

I wake to paint, and keep each eye
open, trace the years' interpretations.
The mirror's figure isn't me—after
    the war, my faces blur.

I find myself outside, where sun colors
the world unfolding, a gravel garden path
to follow through the breathing greens. Living
    doesn't have to feel

hard all the time.

Diptych with Anxious Ewes

Way before early, I wake
to a flock on the loose, astray.
I read the moon's slow clock,
night's white face pasted
on the glinting glass. I toss,
jumble the bedding, fumbled head
locked out of dream half-spent.

Sheep bells in the shrubs outside,
under the sill. I slipped the gin,
and so I trip, losing the game.
Mother, oh may I—
red light. Start again.

~~~

Tick, and the air turns on,
a code for breath, or am I scripting
thin twists, sheet between my knees,
drama-jangled ankles, wrists?
Hitchcock without suspense,
voice caught, stuck like a knuckle,
a bottle cap, a rusty nail.

Where's the wether? Minute,
minute, tock walking
a grinding gait. Again, the bleating—
await with tilting guilt.
I wilt, lost in the baa,
no tale to tell, no peep, no sleep.

In Our Winter Colors

Nights when I don't fit my skin,
worry I left my old selves
in the boxes given to Good Will,

I think of the Silver Cloud Hotel,
where I could book a room alone,
my own tower with a freshly made bed,

become both Rapunzel and the witch
as I sit downstairs at Jimmy's Bar
with a martini and no clothes to fold,

an abstract painting on one wall,
not like the ocean pounding against its frame
when I was a girl in December.

Some days I need marriage by numbers,
paints to match the shape of us,
help me tame the shadows,

paint a door we both can enter,
share an apple from the ochre bowl.
to blend and bring our best colors to light—

whether sienna or Venetian red
will smooth the rough patches,
how deep is the blue for calm water.

Artists call their rose madder fugitive
to mean it elopes with time or light.
Some days, I'm fading—but I do not leave.

Self-Portrait, if I Were Matisse

Let out the fierce in me, orange heat
and the savage green jungle that grows
in my gut. Put on the paint bold,
           a slash, a sweep. Contrast

attracts and repels. Beauty holds
more than one face, and I'll leave
Helen to her own symmetry. I'm looking
           to the heart's red house.

I want the surface below my skin,
the light behind my ears. Primary,
primeval. The color waves to the eye,
           tells the belly now.

I'm serious.
           Play is everything.

Blue Rushing

If I say buffet, only wind blew, if bluster, no bravado,
long wave of cresting, crashing, cresting
wind stripping us down to our nerves,
our tossed, our scoured words,

if now gusts rustle me unraveled as when the trades
shoved in, if knowing we'd go in the morning, already
pulling apart from that place, dusk pushing
blue to black, if it falls

fast in the tropics, if we, unable to anchor in sleep,
pitched across meridians, not hearing in that
howling our own tenderness, our dreaming,
not yet our ticket back—

Forecast, Pacific, Honeymoon

Wind wracking the water
streaming that way, this,
the hard hull shifting.

We watched the weather fax
inch out, watched air drape
a storm, coil into gale force bashing

the Bat Islands. I hunkered in flux,
the frozen past and any
seas ahead uncertain.

When we anchored one night
in Nicaragua, did you notice
a boat listing to its port side?

Lashed together, we entered
the country only to leave
across the no-man's land,

a margin witnessed,
bus ride toward the cloud forest.

Between Life with You and a Week Alone

Having kissed you good bye at 5 a.m.,
chaste in the Departures lane,
I pull into home, gravel under tires,
swing the worn gate open wide

where breathing smells like morning from the country
of my childhood, the night's damp scents
nesting in the grasses, clinging
to roots as light warms a trace
of sage, the memory of apples
or roses, those symbols.

Last day of May, the irises done,
the rest of the yard a rampant eruption—
abundance of emerald and mess—
hard to know where our borders are,
to tell the shape of us—and this young dawn

sends me back to that hillside
above Sharp Road, wind
writing its letters to the willow,
to sky over the pear orchard,

back to the dream of a horse
knee-high in pasture grass,
the red seed heads
bowing from living's weight.

Fatigue floats me down—
each gust on my skin a reminder
I am the woman who stays and longs
to go, life's as green and quick
as the grass, death as certain
as August that dries up the pond.

Self-Portrait, Framed by Bridges, a Vaporetto

Because I grow mostly water, a taste
for salt and hauled by tides, Venice opens
a paradise, Eden glinting green in the current,
    stories under bridges,

echoes in crumbling walls where worn stairways
kneel into brine and trash and passing craft.
The lagoon blooms, a sky. Silvered glass,
    a mirror. Breath, an engine.

Red impatiens in a boat, wisteria draping
a fence. Where color reigns, the sun
rinses each slanting glance, prism or mist,
    the light's palette fished

by Titian—and now I am drowning.

Sketch in Yellow, whether the Sky Looks Blue

You want me to write happy poems,
sunny-side up, but we scramble our eggs.

Yellow through a window, light the cat seeks
as the sun moves him across the floor.

Outside, the Agnes Rose offers blooms
as prim as a grandmother's handkerchief

in this year we did not drive north to see
the last of the daffodils, the tulip fields.

Buttercups make me think of cows
and admonition. Dandelions dot the yard

in gold, in wish, this afternoon hour
that gilds the cedars and chimney bricks,

the universe of plums shining heavy
in the leaves until crows come hunger-drunk.

When the moon rises full and yellow
like the sun's cousin, we think of harvest,

stare into its eye to find ourselves
or the wide Sea of Tranquility

before the tides in us curl toward the coast
mapped on our bodies, the atlas of our past.

How to make peace with summer's decline—
each time a truce, as though we had a choice?

Soon yellow will flame again as trees tower
like bonfires, and this is my happy poem.

ii. wind's parables

I Lose Track of the Variables

Say stress to test how wood
or bone will fail, fatigue
for cracks in steel. What breaks
by degrees—a simple math.

The small worries lodge
in my body's nests, where neck
marries shoulder to skull,
sure pockets of last week
lingering, a shoulder hunched,
a wrist pinched, tension circling

the space between our surfaces.
Some days as long
as the no-man's land
we walked between borders.

How to ease our boundaries,
our words unfolding
after the fiercest spring winds
have stripped the tulips.

Osmosis haunts, crosses
this diaphanous membrane—
what we voice, what's swallowed
when we say *weary* and mean *you*,
no and mean *home*.

How to know which straw's
the last, slanting
in winter light to settle?

We bring our angers, our hands empty.
We bring our translations,
hunt for the formula,
tempered by our years.

We chart the distance between stars
in light years and angles.
The telescope opened the night's world,
a closer look at the stories,
new truths to prove.

Remember the loaf and fish
that increased beyond counting?
Abundance means not measuring.
Trust means you don't have to test.

Collage with One White Anemone

a forecast for wind to blow across this sun

gusts in the trees   a ladder leans against the west side

broom holds up the eastern wall

all day a knocking   thuds of ghosts

or construction outside

refrigerator growl

the road south to Naalehu   wind painting rain on our faces

we drove talk into new landscapes

our letters to each other in the car   Dear I can tell you anything

the road listened   the tires loved the long saddle road

where there was no road

that part of my heart open   the balance

hidden in a box behind the shoes

Has Particle Physics Explained This?

If time can be defined by light,
each minute becomes a wave
pounding the beach at Manzanita
where combers curl and thunder
like furious horses. Wind carries the sand,
a symbol for glass, which invites
the light through. Grit bites.
The shore sticks to our feet, hitches
between our toes, ready
to outstay its welcome.
You don't like the sand.

I'll tell you a secret—
I don't either, or finding it in my shoes
six months later, but Love, I love
the way it glistens near the tideline,
surf hammering as I stand
at the edge where water laps and see
clear to the start of sky.

Collage with Walking and Ice

the wind's parables   the rain that understands

leaves skitter across asphalt

autumn rattles down

we walk with no radio and then we talk

flights up the water tower

across the city a full-circle view

steel steps echo descending   gravity helps

words nest

                    weeds conquer cracks in the stairs

green fingers from crumbling cement

I wear melancholy   scarf of marsh and stone

you keep sun in your blue eyes

dusk a wing home to roost   bird perched behind the moon

back through the gate and the door   ice in glasses

the ease of electric light

Our Bodies Given up for Light

An inch no longer measured by a thumb,
a foot for walking only—
old artifacts abandoned.

Particle and wave, what is the shape
of essential undulations
to which distance now is tethered, and time?

Its lambent body pummels me from the sun,
glistening minutes
shattered on the sand.

What is the shape of love?
Like a turtle pressing
slowly toward the lettuce,

a smooth river stone—or is it the river,
so often standing in for time
rushing over the rocks

like the horse galloping across a field—
or is it riding the horse, the wind in her mane,
in your hair, almost like flying?

Is love a peach, the fuzz a soft burr
in your hand? Or can you not hold love,
the fog that runs through your fingers?

Collage with Buckeyes, Other Signs of Autumn

on the sidewalk split husks   brown shiny buttons

one red leaf drifted into parsley

pasta made with only yolks   pot of marinara

all afternoon scent of tomatoes and warmth

a bottle of red wine in red sauce   a bottle at the table

other years a yellow Penske truck   white line south to California

load of chairs and tables   mahogany you smoothed

blanket wrapped and strapped

you drove   I watched for curves

steep grade warnings   the bear crossing

moths blizzard of bodies and wings

Ashland a break in the Siskiyous

Redding a stop at the Liquor Barn

dusk came close to Red Bluff

oak silhouettes and the sky falling   flat chance to exhale

lights and the exit ramp ahead

How We Are Living

The Nobel Prize in Physics 2016 was divided, one half awarded to David J. Thouless, the other half jointly to F. Duncan M. Haldane and J. Michael Kosterlitz *"for theoretical discoveries of topological phase transitions and topological phases of matter"*. — nobelprize.org

Suddenly a state I never dreamed of,
and *topological phase*
makes me think of mountains
shifting into clouds,
but that's a different kind of map—
I'm hearing about this, not

ice or water, steam wreathing the skin
of the woman after her bath
in pastels by Degas,
but years before you saw me,
scientists wrote about a stage
beyond that matter triad, the tones

between the piano's black and white keys,
a slimming flatter than flapjack,
bug-on-the-windshield splat,
like that night we drove
through a dusk of wings as thin
as ghosts on the road to Red Bluff—

the radio says *quantum computing*,
much faster calculations,
the way an express train speeds past
while the local jolts along
as we're rushing away from our birth,
away from that fall we met

and, years after, our first kiss (oh,
that first long kiss on the dance floor
that changed the state of everything,
someone strumming a washboard),
three cars merging into my lane,
the trees changing orange to red to rain.

Collage with Wheels and Foghorn, Salt All Over

sloped boulders where we sat against

the letter of the law   skittered pebbles into the sound

the year we walked through forest   a clearing for an orchard

grass to our knees

tanager in the apple branches' net   leaves a school of dusty fish

the year we walked the beach to the bay

walked uphill past the Congregational Church

the year we bottled someone else's wine

listened to the ballgame   the car our only radio

the dry-dock year we rode bicycles with wind   the flavors of rain

the loud years and later mornings   year of Thanksgiving

year of martinis and coq au vin   when we could still get a kitchen

deer out front rabbits on the lawn

light talking to the water   haze to the west   the other

islands hard to see

Canada across the strait   in the dark a constellation

the years we looked up   stars piled the night deep

Long after Twenty

Say *cherry, gave my love a*—
say *smoke*, as it follows beauty
that shadows age, pegs we hang our hats on
when we fumble in
from the sun-smitten afternoon.

We've left those other decades
under our pillows,
in the nightstand drawer
that sticks now, just a bit,

and savor everlasting, the idea
of jasmine at other latitudes,
watch our worries hover
above the porch light, feather-soft,
dust-soft, beyond our circumference.

iii. of a feather

Sketch in Blue with Darker Water

I found a feather from a Steller's jay,
left it, let it stay on our front stairs.

Now the weather opens other rooms,
chapel-ceiling fresco cloud encircled.

West, the sky looks more like sea,
steely tide swelling toward the hills.

You worry when my waves of blue
come crashing, knock me back hard.

I read Maggie Nelson's *Bluets*, heard
another woman sing *a small blue thing*.

To paint the dragon on the Chinese plate
the cobalt's mined, crushed, melted.

On some days, blue's the garden blooming
past the porch, a path through forget-me-nots,

a Parrish dusk plunging into night
deeply and translucent blue.

Some days, I am ground and sintered,
set adrift on the lake's grayer shades

lapping into black, where I look down,
down, hear you calling from the shore.

Self-Portrait with a Pitcher

No Vermeer here, but clear glass,
ice a music, mystery when I played young.
Images fall first like bad notes
        bowed from a violin,

rosin, resin, timbre a hollow taunting.
My heart's a shell after the ocean left.
My throat wants and wants, hungers for nothing,
        thirst its own art.

Each new shade a dull betrayal.
I miss how the garden should look in my hands,
feathered green, light poured through water—
        my eyes leave gaps,

a noted absence of birds.

Having Made My Beds

Under March skies, palette shifting white to blue,
I arm with steel, rusty teeth, hack, attack the thickets—
no prince in search of kisses. From one stick—sucker—
grows a rose, cane and thorn
                   a bitter plenty, brief bud.

Oh, cloud of my neglect—fierce bluster surges
to there and here, battle for light, a tangle.
                             More is *more*.

I rooted rugosas, ramblers. *More* grew rampant, followed
blooms into my body under my skin, my tender, my night.
From that one vision, an empire.
                       And I no longer fit.

~~~

How my garden strays—wanton, beads from seed pods split,
spilt jewels lacing soil? A green ocean sinks,
wave after wave sucked from swells,
                       jetsam thrown in the bin.

Shoulders arched above the shed, giants through the roof
died and more grew over dead wood. This madness too much—
Have I given the ghost his due, given up?
                      Where is my creature?

I thought I'd tame these green beasts, train increase into blushing
lapdogs, tender pets, petals panting with summer's drama.
I submit. Doubt
               falls to my hand, another cut.

~~~

Saw bites limb, the fine dust another exposure.
Slow, my progress. The hummingbird zips the yard,
                              chides me from the lilac.

I reach, lean, grit my teeth, dead twigs like talons.

When canes leaf out it's too late—thick wall without pattern,
shrubs knotting a net. Clouds occlude the sun, then leave,
light to dark. Work goes on,
                              the one sure thing.

Those years I wanted roses, and those I turned away, sick
of thorn bite, green riot—wait until they open.
Then the vision missed, lost in wilderness
                              grown too wild.

~~~

I thought the flowers proof, a history plotted, castle rapt,
saw my own stories flourish, summer's heat a veil
and welcome, overstayed. Now I cut
                              a maze I can reckon,

hitch another hour to my hands, bag of stickers dragged.
These fierce cousins bite too feral for a bouquet
and still it hurts to clip the tender green,
                              blunt such vigor.

The sun runs short and thin, thyme dry in winter's teeth,
some of the rosemary dead. I head through this year shorn
of fleece and swank, too drunk to drink,
                              too old to think it pretty.

~~~

Plant me no wild roses, no Nootka, musk,
no swollen thickets, star mantle pinking the hill.

Calm me with no omens blooming. Morning brings
its own prayers, potluck, from sky
                              to this plain table.

Done with thorn clouds billowing, my tastes have changed from wild,
from worse. Don't bury me
                    under briars called romantic.

I'll tell, keep leaves and other arts for other eyes,
fingers sharp with skill. Still, sun rules the sky.
I save a love for wild things,
                    and in the night, terrors.

Self-Portrait with Crows

Wings wipe the sky, smear and gone,
leave the raw caw cry behind,
a fluid composition after rain
     rinses the high gray,

a day smudged, flood by light diffused,
no shadows but these black rags,
murder witness spelled across the canvas,
     incantation canted.

Tricksters in triplicate, carbon copies crease
oil shades I blotch below my eyes.
See the years fly, feathers brushing
     up against the fence,

the dead tree left.

Five Tries to Say I'm Sorry

Only one year I planted pumpkins—
shell for keeping very well, or golden carriage.

I've never been a good Cinderella,
but I've wanted happily ever

and long for the country called leisure,
feel you closest when we're gone.

I don't like to travel—but remember
those days after the dash for the airport,

dragging our baggage to carry on,
the small home with the red roof (*casita*,

as though another language made
the walls exotic) dusk early and the notes

the yellow windows wrote, no grocery lists,
lights grinning up the palms, and then stars?

Here in a house where tasks
are meant to add up to romance,

my hands twist, slacken, can't find
the name for what I want, can't ask.

Daily I revise myself, redraft my chapters.
I've been hunting for my heart

and it isn't in the television, the lump
of laundry left undone.

You tell the story you want to hear.
This is the best love letter I can write.

In the Country Called Marriage

The sky's an orchard, peach harvest
of another morning we peel and swallow,
a cure for yesterday's mistakes—
my doubts in blue cotton dresses,
the watch running backwards.

Every year's another tree we sleep under
while cows in the pasture doze and chew,
the horse shifts her weight, and sparrows
hide from the heat, myself a bird that flew
out of my attic, the whole flock of me fleeing.

With a better sense of direction, I could draw
a map for you, chart north or a kind of peace
like the climbing rose where finches perch,
and I might build a nest of me.

Dawn or dusk—that cusp opens a door
to the day's temporal meadows of rue
and surprise or the night's hushed assurance
when we sit together, the porch light unmasking
snow falling or the finest rain.

Sketch in Red with Rust

Spring makes us wake with robins,
red in the hedge, flannel scraps in the leaves,

dawn spilling across the east
as each day makes a new map,

clouds of Japanese maple aflame in sunlight,
low azalea waves, the crocosmia you love,

cherry tomatoes we imagine
when we sink starts in dark soil,

the stack of bricks out back,
broken terra cotta pots where roses tangle,

blood shushing a song of air and iron,
the body conducting its systolic symphony,

blunt notice that every day makes us older,
further from a home in the country—

red barn, red door on the blue house,
the neighbor's rooster screeching in the morning,

a truck after the dust is washed off,
and the sky's end as we'd ride into town

for more gradations: glass of cabernet,
clutch of poppies, shiny ruby shoes.

Five Scenes

If it's the quick spin out of town, car chasing the desert,
white streak with the top down, red vinyl seats,
three on the tree, one hand on the wheel while evening dusts
my arms, the stars promise. The engine sings. Chrome shines like
  teeth.

If it's the '30s, I'm a character actress leaving the city.
The studio cheats. The director throws the dice. I gamble,
sick of doing what I'm told. You're working late, but we
have plans. The hotel key fits the lock like good sex.

If the suite is a plain set, a scene in white and black,
yellow splashes make me think of lemons—in a tumbler.
If whippet statues guard the gate, I'll be a princess,
room service my court, the fountain a viceroy with good advice.

If the wind is Myrna Loy, decked out in feathers, gliding
down the stairs, plays the garden's leaves like a symphony
or a cabaret, virtues tossed in the heated pool as ice melts
in a heavy glass and shadows float their last hours.

If I slip into night like a cat through a fence, silk sliding
over shoulders, the moon tells only half the story.
Gin's oblivion scripts the rest, the dark heat a door waiting
for you to knock. The road that brought us here will take us back.

Sketch in Green Grown Close

Any green grass can hold a horse,
but only a crow grazes on the parking strip,

the garden this year fending for itself—
the rambling rose's flood of thorns, the sage

not naiveté or cash or envy
sneaking emerald in the weeds,

not the theater's green room where I ate
green grapes before the show,

costume of my Augusts gasping
across the Hudson from New York.

Old oaks and maples choked with leaves,
held the heat close before we moved

west between these laurels, walls shoving
toward the sun, hedges I dread to trim,

but you climb the ladder I'm grabbing
as counterbalance, confetti falling

green around me, scents of honey, vanilla,
then the rake and broom until done,

clutching our green—a road trip
to our salad days, a bottle of wine from Sousa,

the green light that paints the dusk's edges
before night falls completely.

At the Desert Hotel

I write myself out the door
early into the jasmine,
white roses grown to trace
the garden's swept edges.

I left my slack dreams
in a glass of water, left my sleep
on the bed, my body's map
stamped on the sheets, a poem for you.

Flown to where the fountain sings,
I untie the knots in my throat
one-by-one down to my chest.
I breathe just enough.

The moments alone, moments together,
easy meaning a morning
paper, coffee, the sun
collecting its brushes and knives

to paint the hours, noon and after,
green fronds played by the wind.
I want to hear the visions, find the lines.
Shadows ripple blue, and I am lost.

Dusk unwraps like a package.
I join you at this little table,
push words around
like so many tender bites.

We arrive at our best
in the country called Leisure—
salted almonds, ice in tumblers.
Lights climb the palms.

We sip through evening,
listen to the night's dry music.
The fountain makes its own song,
the water its own bed.

Kind of Love

I want to love you unbuffered as a summer storm
        unbuttons the trees, to sweep you and sweep.

I want to love you like the calm after the gust
        when small bird symphonies scrape the sky
        in the towering tulip tree.

I want to love you like windfall apples gathered
        for pie, love you latticed, with steam.

I want to love you before the clock's first word and mid-
        sentence and full stop and begin again.

I want to love you the way the comb runs
        through hair time after time
        over time unsnarling.

I want to love you with spangles in my hair
        and road maps in the glove box.

May I love you bedeviled, bemused—may your
        bewilderment be my welcome mat,

love you like the sand's consolation
        at low tide, and like the ocean, flecked
        and galloping, driven panting to the shore,

love you the way starfish stick to the rocks,
        all arm and mouth.

On the Desire Line

Damn hunger hunkering
down, hankering,
        a soft-pawed beast

when the lemon trees,
the window called *hither*
            —and I could not.

Swallowed, I swallowed madness,
bad when I cried to be good.

Head emptied, my hands
implied agreement.

My fingers murmured.
Water whispered. Thirst

argued amnesia—
            more
                        and more
melted into less.

~~~

For a known language
and a few leaves crumpled,

I unfold myself, a stretched
rest, another morning.

The sunlight sallies, hot
bravado—this isthmus

between outcomes

                    to choose
                                to change,
                                          to feel all my skin.

What the wind says—hurry.
The sun—wait,

silence like silk unrolling.
What the heat says—now.

Trees talk among themselves.

Flutters in clipped hedges.
                    Air so dry
                                it scours our lungs.

Little mazes cross
                    the lawn, skirt the palms,
                                the fountains.

Let me be
                    mysterious here
                                and forgiven.

~~~

Straight across, the road cuts
until it finds the mountain's flank.

Details blur. I covet bliss
                    and thwart myself—

want the shortest path
to link two longings.

Desire travels ahead
as true as the crows.

Of a feather, we sit slaked
by light and each other,

a wet song in the throat.

Far from what we know, we pretend—
      if this were life
           in the lap of it,

vast and barren, dry without sorrow.
      How Italian!

Sun on my tongue and a lemon
      in hand for light.
             The blue sky rises.

Sketch in Purple with Every Dusk a Garden

Our lilac towers, leans across the path,
a branch to knock us on the head.

Five years we waited for it to bloom.
Now its ten thousand flowers open,

tiny cups to catch the certain rain
until heavy branches bend,

a low-slung bower, scent a twilight—brief
then rinsed away, its season done.

True, purple was the color for kings and priests,
a dye fashioned from snails, and therefore rare,

but what of violet, tending toward blue,
the shadows in snow, when we had snow?

Hydrangeas shade toward one or the other—
does it matter which, this pressure to be right?

Grapes look purple, but we call wine red
before it stains our lips, our tongues.

The scientists say nothing's colored true—
it's just the brain's interpretation.

Take two steps along the spectrum
and perspective shifts. In the alley,

money plants blossom before the seed coins,
a weed to remind us we are rich.

If I Were the Woman

After La Terrasse à Préfailles, *by Henri Lebasque, 1922*

When she climbs alone the red-dirt hill,
her back to the sea's blue comment,

ignoring lovers pressed on the shore
by the falling sun, flattened in the distance
like birds that leave flying for tomorrow.

Day drapes her shoulders, ochre
as the sail on the bay's one boat.

After she closes the garden's gate, she walks
the right half of the path's ring,

and if I were the woman climbing that hill
above the lawn's shadows, the heat seeping away,
I'd be coming up to sit with you,

our table on the terrace, the wine a night
poured as that sky swallows us whole.

Be My Nest

Lowering, the sun lit and limned
each wavelet, glitter water tugging me
toward the line between sky
and sound, the farther islands where
we've never landed,

just the ferry here in summer,
this hill above the channel and the small house
a night or two our refuge, our belonging
to each other and this shore—

and if on the boat over I carry
other years and ask again
how could we stay, what is the work
we'd do here, the living for the living,
and then the work of marriage—

under calling from the rustling green
cedars, firs, black locusts home
to chirp, trill, or screech, I let
those questions dart as lightly
as the hummingbird that hovers,

rests, chides from a bush
beside the path, and the bird
in my chest tucks its head,
floats on this evening without wind
as tide out, tide in,
the currents running north.

Acknowledgments

The following poems, or earlier versions of them, first appeared in the following journals:

Cascadia Review: "On the Desire Line"
The Chaffin Journal: "How We are Living," "Sketch in Purple with Every Dusk a Garden"
Cider Press Review: "Having Made My Beds," "Five Tries to Say I'm Sorry"
Cirque: "Appetites," "Another Supper Finds Me Lost," "Self-Portrait, Framed by Bridges, a *Vaporetto*"
Earth's Daughters: "Self-Portrait, if I Were Bonnard"
Escapism: "Five Scenes," "Collage with One White Anemone"
Floating Bridge Review: "Self-Portrait with an Aubade"
Glass: "Sketch in Blue with Darker Water"
Hubbub: "Time and Materials"; "Diptych with Limited Symptoms," "Sketch in Yellow, whether the Sky Looks Blue"
Off the Coast: "Between Life with You and a Week Alone," "Has Particle Physics Explained This?"
Pacifica Literary Review: "I Lose Track of the Variables"
Pirene's Fountain: "This Shade So Early Clings"
Santa Fe Literary Review: "Diptych with Anxious Ewes"
StringTown: "Sketch in Red with Rust" (forthcoming)
Tulane Review: "Self-Portrait, if I Were Matisse"
Valparaiso Poetry Review: "Self-Portrait with Crows"

My heartfelt thanks to the members of my writing group who helped me through many of these poems: Eileen Duncan, Pat Hurshell, Sigrun Susan Lane, Anne Pitkin, Judith Skillman, and Martha Vallely.

Thanks are due Nancy Anderson, Claire Kervran, and Bonnie Garmus, and to others who generously read this manuscript in its various versions and provided insightful critiques and much-needed encouragement. Thanks also to Ravenna Press for their continued support.

Finally, deep gratitude to my entire family for their love and patience.

About the Author

Joannie Stangeland is the author of several collections of poetry. Her work has also appeared in numerous journals, including *Cimarron Review*, *Prairie Schooner*, and *The Southern Review*. Joannie lives in Seattle, where she works as a technical writer and helps out at the family winery.